Earthquakes

Earthquakes

Trudi Strain Trueit

$\mathscr{Watts}$ LIBRARY™

Franklin Watts
A Division of Scholastic Inc.
New York • Toronto • London • Auckland • Sydney
Mexico City • New Delhi • Hong Kong
Danbury, Connecticut

For Brian and the children of the Pacific Rim

Note to readers: Definitions for words in **bold** can be found in the Glossary at the back of this book.

Photographs © 2003: AP/Wide World Photos: 18 (Aaron Favila), 39 (Katsumi Kasahara), 46 (Burhan Ozbilici), 43 (Reed Saxon), 8 (Mark J. Terrill), 6 (Chiaki Tsukumo), 10 (Nick Ut), 22 (Walt Zeboski), 25, 30, 35, 40, 47; Bernard Adnet: 17; Corbis Images: cover (AFP), 15 (Dave Bartruff), 27 top (Bettmann), 5 left, 27 bottom (Lloyd Cluff), 37 (Enny Nuraheni), 44, 48 (Roger Ressmeyer), 26 (Michael S. Yamashita), 36; Getty Images/David McNew/Newsmakers: 2; Photri Inc.: 12, 13, 16, 23; Tom Bean: 5 right, 14.

The photograph on the cover shows a buckled road in Taiwan following an earthquake there.
The photograph opposite the title page shows a large earthquake fault on the north side of Mammoth Mountain in California.

Library of Congress Cataloging-in-Publication Data

Trueit, Trudi Strain.
    Earthquakes / Trudi Strain Trueit.
       p. cm. — (Watts library)
    Includes bibliographical references and index.
    ISBN 0-531-12197-6 (lib. bdg.)   0-531-16243-5 (pbk.)
    1. Earthquakes—Juvenile literature. I. Title. II. Series.
QE521.3 .T78 2003
551.22—dc21   2002006150

Contents

This twisted section of the Hanshin Expressway was just part of the damage done by the Kobe earthquake of January 1995.

Chapter One

Moment of Terror

It happened in the quiet, early-morning hours of January 17, 1995. The thriving port city of Kobe, Japan, was just waking up when the jolt hit. The shallow **earthquake**, located 6 miles (10 kilometers) beneath the seafloor, rumbled through Kobe with devastating results. Cracks formed through cement foundations, turning homes and businesses into clouds of rubble. Skyscrapers waved from side to side before toppling like dominoes. The quake even flipped part of a freeway.

Similar Quakes, Different Outcomes

The Kobe quake occurred exactly one year to the day and at nearly the same time a similar quake ripped through Northridge, California. On January 17, 1994, a 6.8-magnitude earthquake struck the Los Angeles suburb, killing fifty-six people and damaging twenty thousand buildings. Compared to Northridge, ten times as many buildings were damaged in Kobe and the death toll was one hundred times higher. Some critics charged that the city of Kobe was poorly prepared for the disaster, and the situation worsened when the Japanese government initially refused help from other countries.

The quake, which moved the ground 7 inches (18 centimeters) in places, damaged nearly 200,000 buildings, along with 60 percent of Kobe's bridges. In less than twenty seconds, the 6.8-**magnitude** (or strength) earthquake shook the land within a 60-mile (96-km) radius. The shock leveled the equivalent of seventy U.S. city blocks. In a city of 1.4 million people, more than 5,500 were killed, and one-fifth of Kobe's population was left homeless. Damages topped $100 billion after the worst quake to hit the area in nearly fifty years.

Did You Feel That?

About once every thirty seconds, an earthquake rumbles through the planet. Most of them cause minor shaking, or **tremors**, that are too weak for you to feel. Earthquakes are vibrations that occur when energy is released from rocks within Earth. The vibrations are energy in the form of waves that move through rock and shake the ground. Earthquakes may be caused by human activity, such as coal miners setting off explosions as they tunnel deep below ground. Erupting volcanoes, impacting meteorites, landslides, or underground water pressure may also spark them. But most often, it is movement within Earth's crust that is to blame for jostling the ground.

Across the globe, places like Japan, China, Iran, Turkey, Peru, Chile, and Mexico are hot spots for earthquakes. In the United States, California and Alaska are frequent targets, but they aren't the only places where Earth quivers. **Seismologists**, scientists who study earthquakes, estimate that about 90 percent of the U.S. population lives in areas considered to be at some risk for seismic, or quake, activity. *Seismos* is a Greek word meaning "shock."

In this book, you'll explore what sets off earthquakes and why some areas more likely to shudder than others. You'll learn how scientists detect, measure, and study earthquakes in an effort to someday be able to accurately forecast them. You'll also learn how you can prepare in case planet Earth decides to shake up your life.

Movers and Shakers

Although millions of earthquakes will occur across the globe this year, only about 500,000 will be strong enough to be picked up by instruments. Of those, nearly 100,000 will be felt by humans and 150 will cause serious injury and damage.

Quake Felt 'Round the World

The collapse of each of the World Trade Center towers on September 11, 2001, shook the ground with the force of two minor earthquakes, registering magnitudes of 2.1 and 2.3 on the Richter scale.

Sixteen people were killed in January 1994 when an earthquake in Northridge, California, caused the collapse of this apartment building.

Chapter Two

On Shaky Ground

When the walls begin to sway and the windows rattle, it may seem as if the world is being suddenly shocked into motion. But, Earth is actually a fiery planet that is constantly changing beneath your feet. If you could slice into Earth, you would discover three main layers: the **crust**, the **mantle**, and the **core**.

At the center of the planet, more than 3,900 miles (6,300 km) from the surface, lies the core. Made mainly of iron and nickel, the core has two layers: the outer

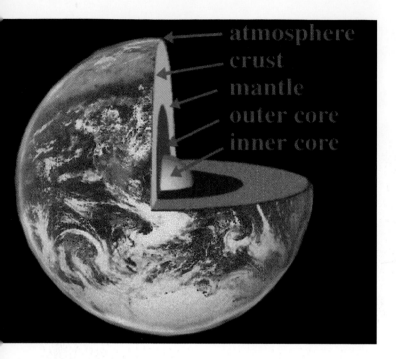

atmosphere
crust
mantle
outer core
inner core

This artist's cutaway view of Earth's interior shows the planet's different layers.

core and the inner core. Scientists estimate that the liquid outer core is almost as hot as the surface of the Sun, about 9,000° F (5,000° C). The inner core probably reaches temperatures above 12,000° F (6,600° C), yet it remains solid. The massive weight of the layers above it keeps the iron and nickel in the inner core from melting.

The mantle, a layer of rock softened by heat, surrounds the core. The mantle extends from about 30 miles (50 km) below the surface to a depth of 1,800 miles (2,900 km). It makes up almost 70 percent of Earth's total mass. In Earth's mantle, temperatures ranging from 950° to 7,500° F (500° to 4,150° C) keep the soft rock moving very slowly in giant currents.

Above the mantle sits Earth's outermost rocky layer, called the crust. The crust is divided into pieces, much like a cracked eggshell. There are eight large sections, or **tectonic plates**, and many smaller ones. Tectonic plates may support continents, islands, oceans, or any combination of the three. All of North America, much of the Arctic Circle, and part of the Atlantic Ocean sit on the North American Plate. The Pacific plate is the largest chunk of crust. It stretches nearly 9,000 miles (14,400 km), supporting most of the Pacific Ocean.

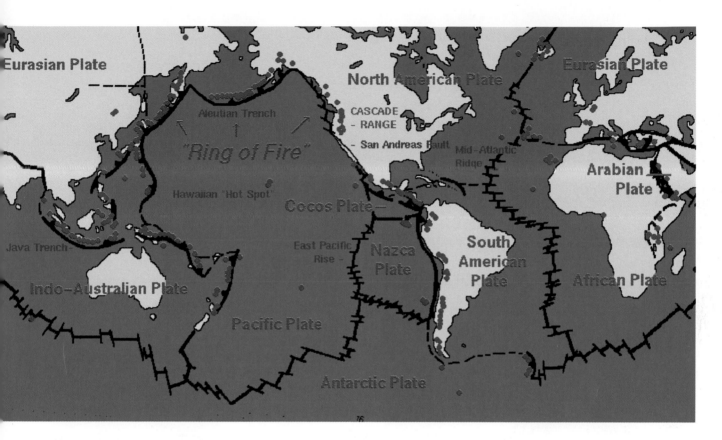

Eurasian Plate

North American Plate

Eurasian Plate

Aleutian Trench

CASCADE
- RANGE

San Andreas Fault

Mid-Atlantic
Ridge

Arabian
Plate

"Ring of Fire"

Hawaiian "Hot Spot"

Cocos Plate—

Java Trench-

East Pacific
Rise -

Nazca
Plate

South
American
Plate

African Plate

Indo-Australian Plate

Pacific Plate

Antarctic Plate

76

Finding Fault

Earth's tectonic plates are always in motion, fueled by the hot currents in the mantle below. The plates travel at an average rate of 0.5 to 3 inches (2 to 8 cm) per year, or about as fast as your fingernails grow. On their journey, they may scrape, collide, spread apart, or move past each other, creating cracks in Earth's crust called **faults**. Over a long period of time, perhaps hundreds of years, the stress of rock pushing against rock builds until it must be released. The rock splits, either along an existing fault or along a newly formed fault, sending shock waves through the ground—an earthquake! The tremor may

This map shows Earth's major tectonic plates and volcanoes. The Ring of Fire is an area of particularly intense seismic and volcanic activity.

The San Andreas fault is in California. It is 600 miles (970 km) long and marks the spot where the Pacific Plate and North American Plate meet.

be so slight that only the most sensitive instruments can detect it. Or it may be far more intense, causing injury and damage at the surface of Earth.

More than 90 percent of earthquakes occur near where two or more tectonic plates meet, because these boundaries are where most faults are located. But faults can be found anywhere in the crust. Any time there is movement along a fault, an earthquake is the result.

A fault may be as small as a few inches or may stretch for thousands of miles. It may be close to the surface, causing visible cracks, or it may be quite deep and hidden from view. Along a fault, the split sections of rock slide in opposite directions, either vertically, horizontally, or at an angle.

The San Andreas Fault, located where the Pacific and North American Plates meet, is one of the most famous

fault zones in the world. Its boundaries stretch from southern California's Imperial Valley to the north, 600 miles (1,000 km) along the Pacific Coast. The San Andreas Fault can be seen clearly from the air as it slices through rivers, deserts, roads, and mountains. In some places, the fault is 10 miles (16 km) deep. Sections of the fault are to blame for more than twenty major earthquakes in the last century, including an 8.3 in magnitude quake that hit San Francisco in 1906 and a 7.1 in magnitude jolt that occurred during the World Series in October of 1989. The World Series quake killed sixty-seven people, destroyed 100,000 buildings, and collapsed a 30-foot (9-meter) section of the Bay Bridge, which connects San Francisco to Oakland.

The Cypress Freeway Structure in San Francisco could not withstand the force of the earthquake that struck that city in October 1989.

15

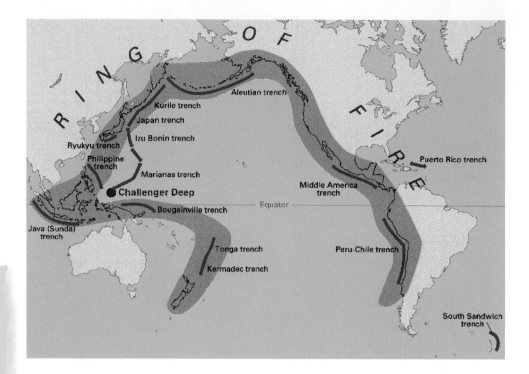

Calm Continents

No spot is earthquake-proof, but earthquakes are less likely to occur in places that are well inside a tectonic plate, such as Australia, Antarctica, or southern Africa. In the United States, Florida, South Dakota, Wisconsin, and Iowa are the states that have the fewest quakes.

Hot Zones

More than 80 percent of the world's earthquakes are centered in an area called the **Circum-Pacific Belt**. This is where several plates, including the massive Pacific Plate, border each other. It's also known as the Ring of Fire because of the extensive volcanic and earthquake activity that occurs along its boundaries. The Ring of Fire extends 24,000 miles (38,000 km) from the west coast of South America and north through Mexico, California, the Pacific Northwest, western Canada, and Alaska. It then stretches eastward across the Aleutian Islands to Asia and Japan, and then dips south to include the Philippines, New Guinea, and New Zealand.

Another earthquake zone follows the border of the

Sisters of Fire

On February 28, 2001, a 6.8-magnitude quake rattled Kobe's sister city, Seattle, Washington. The earthquake injured four hundred people and caused $5 billion in damage. But scientists say this quake was just a jiggle compared to the "big one" that is to come. Like Kobe, Seattle sits on the Ring of Fire. The Pacific Northwest lies close to where the 1,000-mile (1,600-km) long Juan de Fuca Plate borders the North American Plate. Right now, scientists think that the two plates are locked tightly together. But someday, when the stress becomes too much, the energy will likely be released in a giant quake that could top 9.0 in magnitude.

Eurasian Plate. The **Alpide Belt** moves north from Java and Sumatra into China's Himalaya Mountains. It spans west from there, cutting through Iran, Iraq, and Turkey to the Mediterranean Sea and, finally, to the Atlantic Ocean. About 17 percent of the planet's earthquakes occur along the Alpide belt.

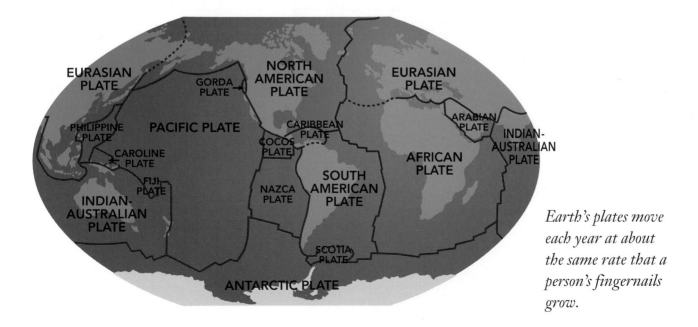

Earth's plates move each year at about the same rate that a person's fingernails grow.

17

Students in the Pacific Island nation of the Philippines perform an earthquake drill. The Philippines are located on the Ring of Fire.

Chapter Three

Sizing Up Shocks

It's a peaceful morning in your classroom. Pencils are scribbling. Minds are calculating or, perhaps, dreaming of lunch. You hardly notice the slight sway and low rumble that feels as if a truck is going past. Suddenly, your notebook slides to the edge of your desk. Your chair scoots forward. The world map on the wall is swinging and the globe topples to the floor. It's an earthquake!

The tremor lasts less than ten seconds, although it feels as if the shaking goes on forever. Yet, while you are huddled under your desk, wondering when the quake will finally end, people hundreds of miles away barely feel the ground hiccup. Why? Every earthquake has a **focus**, the location underground where it begins. The **epicenter** is the point on the surface directly above the focus. The closer you are to the epicenter, the more likely you are to feel the force of the quake.

Energy moves away from the focus in the form of invisible **seismic waves**, or shock waves. There are three types of seismic waves: **P waves**, **S waves**, and **surface waves**. The first shock waves to hit the surface of the planet are primary waves, or P waves. They move the fastest through rock, at speeds of about 4 miles (6 km) per second. P waves compress and stretch

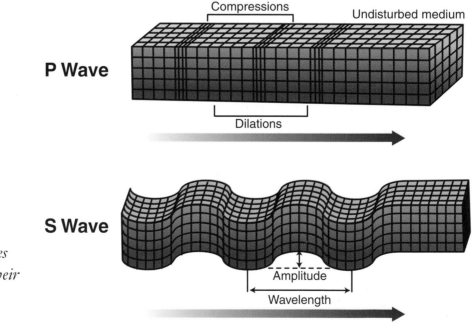

This drawing of the movement of S waves and P waves show their different effects on Earth's surface.

rock as they travel, causing the first jolt that you feel. Secondary waves, or S waves follow the P waves, moving at about 2 miles (3 km) per second. They shake the ground both up and down and also back and forth. S waves may jostle trees, crack buildings, and keep cars from driving in straight lines. Since they move through the entire body of Earth, P and S waves are known as body waves. Surface waves are the slowest waves. They are generated by the P and S waves hitting the surface, forming new energy waves. Surface waves may produce a rolling sensation that feels like waves on the water. Surfaces waves tend to cause the most damage because they strike areas already weakened by P and S waves and can last up to several minutes in the most extreme cases.

Measuring Motion

Chinese philosopher Chang Heng is credited with building the first device to detect tremors. In 132 A.D., he invented the **seismoscope**, a 6 foot (2 m) in diameter bronze urn ringed with dragon heads and frogs. During a quake, a pendulum inside the urn triggered a dragon to drop its ball into the open mouth of a frog below. The frog farthest from the epicenter caught the ball, indicating the direction from which the jolt had come. One time, one of the dragons dropped its ball, although no one had felt a thing. Days later, messengers arrived on horseback with the news that a major quake had struck the Chinese capitol, 400 miles (640 km) away!

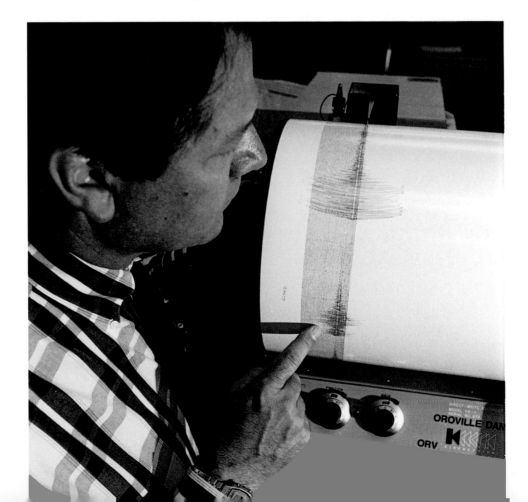

A seismologist studies the readout on a seismograph. This readout is known as a seismogram.

Today, seismologists rely on instruments called **seismographs** to measure seismic waves and determine the magnitude of an earthquake. Seismographs use hanging weights, or pendulums, attached to a solid frame. When the ground shakes, the frame shakes with it, but the weights remain still and record the motion between themselves and the frame. Seismographs were once manual, but information is now measured electronically. The data is sent via radio waves or telephone wires to a pen that records the motion of the waves on magnetic tape or a rotating drum covered with paper. The drum rotates while moving laterally, so the pen can record the seismic waves as zig-zagging lines on the page. The bigger the

Seismographs depict seismic activity as four different kinds of seismograms.

earthquake, the bigger the zig-zags made on the paper. This written record of an earthquake is called a **seismogram**. Modern seismographs can magnify ground motion thousands of times so scientists can see even the slightest tremors.

In the United States, a network of 2,500 seismograph stations report quake data to the United States Geological Survey's National Earthquake Information Center (NEIC) in Golden, Colorado. A central digital computer is able to calculate the focus, epicenter, and initial magni-

Four Major Types of Seismograms

Tectonic like Earthquakes

Shallow Volcanic Earthquakes

Surface Events

Harmonic Tremor

10 Seconds

USGS

tude of the quake (the magnitude may later be increased or decreased based on additional information). Within minutes, the information is sent out via phone lines and space satellites to more than four thousand stations across the globe.

Rating Quivers and Quakes

In 1935, California Institute of Technology professor Dr. Charles Richter came up with a scale to compare the strength of earthquakes. Scientists use the information gathered from seismographs to give each earthquake a numeric rating on the **Richter scale**. The stronger the quake, the higher it is placed on the scale. The Richter scale begins at zero and has no upper limit. Each whole number represents a tenfold increase in ground shaking. A quake rated at magnitude 6.0 has ten times more motion than a 5.0-magnitude tremor and a hundred times more motion than a 4.0-magnitude tremor. No earthquake in human history has ever reached a magnitude of 10 on the scale. The worst quake ever recorded on Earth was 9.5 in magnitude and tore through southern Chile in May of 1960. More than two thousand people were killed and millions were left homeless by the horrific shock.

Richter's original scale had its limitations. A tremor had to occur within 270 miles (600 km) of a particular type of seismograph and within the top 10 miles (16 km) of the planet's crust. This meant that the scale was fairly effective in measuring California quakes, which are usually shallow, but not good for measuring deeper quakes in other places. Seismologists

were able to extend Richter's scale to include quakes any distance from seismograph stations and at depths up to 450 miles (700 km). Eventually, newer, more accurate ways of measuring magnitude were developed.

A bicyclist passes demolished buildings in Kobe, Japan, after the earthquake there in October 1995. The destruction caused by an earthquake is the most visible measurement of an earthquake's magnitude.

Today, the scale most seismologists prefer is called the **moment magnitude scale**, or Mw, scale. Seismologists determine the earthquake's strength, or seismic moment, based on either a mathematical calculation of the fault rupture or from the total energy recorded on a seismogram. Other scales refer to only part of the seismic activity, but moment magnitude looks at the entire seismogram. This makes it a very reliable method for measuring large earthquakes, although it can be used to measure quakes of any size. While the Richter scale placed the 1995 Kobe, Japan, quake at a magnitude of 6.8, according to the moment magnitude scale, the tremor registered 7.0.

Active Alaska

Besides the 9.5-magnitude shaker in Chile, only three other earthquakes have earned a 9.0 or above on the magnitude scale in the last hundred years. All were centered in Alaska, the worst being a 9.2-magnitude earthquake that hit Prince William Sound in 1964. It was the biggest quake ever to shake the United States. The state of Alaska experiences more than half of all of the quakes that strike the nation, and has suffered eight of the top ten

largest quakes in U.S. history. Missouri and California follow Alaska in the ninth and tenth spots.

Exploding Earth

An 8.0-magnitude earthquake packs the punch of more than 1 billion tons of dynamite.

Magnitude scales measure quakes based on the energy released through seismic waves. They do not take into account damage caused on the surface. Two quakes may have the same rating on a magnitude scale, but have very different effects above ground. A 6.8-magnitude tremor centered in the middle of the Atlantic Ocean may not even be felt by humans, while the same size quake in a heavily populated area of China could be disastrous. The kind of soil, types of buildings, and the length of shaking also play a role in determining the amount of destruction caused on the surface.

To measure an earthquake's intensity, or how much damage it has caused, seismologists look to a scale designed by Italian scientist Giuseppe Mercalli. In 1902, before the advent of modern technology, Mercalli relied on eyewitness accounts and damage reports to rate quakes. He used Roman numerals from one to twelve to describe the shaking and devastation. Currently, the United States uses an updated version of the scale, called the **Modified Mercalli Intensity Scale**.

Every earthquake gets just one rating on the magnitude scale, but it may have several ratings on the intensity scale. Zones closer to the epicenter suffer more damage and therefore rate higher on the scale than zones that are further away. Scientists often send out questionnaires to earthquake survivors so they can make an accurate measurement of a quake's intensity.

Comparing Quakes

Modified Mercalli Intensity Scale		Richter Scale		
Description		**Magnitude**	**Category**	**Average Quakes Per Year World wide**
I.	Shaking recorded by instruments, but not felt by people	Less than 3	Very Minor	3,285,000
II.	Shaking is felt only by people at rest, especially those in upper floors of buildings			
III.	People indoors feel a slight vibration, similar to a passing truck; standing cars rock slightly	3 to 3.9	Minor	49,000
IV.	People indoors and outdoors feel vibration; some awakened if it occurs at night. Dishes, windows, and doors shake; walls crack			
V.	Quake felt by nearly everyone; doors swing open, unstable objects fall, and pendulum clocks stop	4 to 4.9	Light	6,200
VI.	Everyone feels quake; plaster and pictures fall, windows and dishes break; people run outside			
VII.	Difficult for people to stand; chimneys crack, large bells ring, waves move on ponds, slight to moderate damage in well-built structures	5 to 5.9	Moderate	800
VIII.	Difficult to drive; chimneys, walls, and statues fall. Furniture overturns, trees break, and considerable damage is caused in well-built structures with partial collapse	6 to 6.9	Strong	120
IX.	People panic, animals run in confusion, and well-built buildings shift off their foundations			
X.	Many structures destroyed, water is thrown out of rivers, and large landslides occur	7 to 7.9	Major	18
XI.	Railroads bend, bridges are destroyed, and few structures remain			
XII.	Total damage occurs to all structures, waves wash ashore, and rivers change course	8 or higher	Great	1

Buckled trolley tracks and uprooted pavement stones on Howard Street in San Francisco were some of the least of the damage caused by the earthquake in that city on April 18, 1906.

Chapter Four

Triggering Disaster

The raw power of a great earthquake can continue to devastate lives and the landscape long after the initial shaking ends. The destruction may go on in the form of **aftershocks**, which are smaller earthquakes that occur near the epicenter for days, weeks, and sometimes years. Earthquakes may also spark landslides, fires, and **tsunamis** (soo-NAH-mees), which are large sea waves. In this chapter, you will explore some of the incredible consequences that can result when planet

Earth decides to tremble, rumble, and roll. The consequences of these seismic adjustments can be seen and felt for centuries.

Shock After Shock

In the early nineteenth century, New Madrid was a growing farming community and port city in the southeastern corner of Missouri. The settlement town of four hundred residents had been built on a ridge of sand and clay, tucked along a winding bend of the busy Mississippi River. But at 2:00 A.M. on December 16, 1811, the city of New Madrid was changed forever.

That morning, a 7.7-magnitude earthquake barreled through the town, toppling chimneys, breaking furniture, and collapsing log homes and barns. The land rolled in waves, opening up large cracks in the surface. The soft banks of the Mississippi River crumbled, and the churning river swallowed ships, homes, and acres of farmland. Walls of water rose in 8-foot (2-m) swells. According to witnesses, the Mississippi actually flowed backward for a time. The shock was felt as far away as Boston, more than 1,000 miles (1,700 km) away.

But it wasn't over. For days and weeks after the major earthquake, the aftershocks kept coming—small tremors, frightening jolts, and terrifying shakers that battered the town again and again. On January 23, 1812, another 7.6-magnitude quake struck, which was followed by a 7.9-magnitude shaker on February 7, 1812.

Scientists estimated that in less than two months, New

Madrid was rocked by more than 1,500 aftershocks. After-shocks are usually caused by minor readjustments along the section of the fault that slipped during the main quake. Usually, the larger the main shock, the larger the aftershocks will be and the longer they will continue.

The numerous shocks that hit the Mississippi Valley not only caused landslides, but also lowered the elevation of the town by as much as 15 feet (4.5 m). Violent ground shaking in an earthquake may cause loosely packed, water-saturated soil near the surface to break apart. In a process called **liquefaction**, soil temporarily loses its strength and acts like fluid, sinking or floating. Liquefaction can be triggered by minor quakes, but is more common in quakes measuring above 5.5 in magnitude. It collapses buildings, freeways, and bridges near coastlines. Earthquakes may also cause wet soil to bubble to the surface and erupt. These tiny, muddy volcanoes are called **sand blows**.

When the aftershocks ended, the Mississippi River's course was changed, new waterfalls and lakes were created, and most of the original settlement of New Madrid was destroyed. The New Madrid seismic zone stretches 120 miles (200 km) and is

Slip Sliding Away

On June 7, 1692, an 8.0-magnitude quake struck Port Royal, Jamaica, with such force that the sandy soil liquefied and sank into the harbor, taking people, buildings, and entire streets down with it. More than 30 percent of the city simply disappeared into the harbor.

still quite active today, although a big shock hasn't occurred for many years. The faults lie buried under sediments a mile (1.6 km) thick. In the event of a big earthquake, seismologists say the soft sediments would allow seismic waves to travel twenty times farther than waves in California. They warn that a strong earthquake will strike again someday, with damage likely occurring over a seven-state area.

City Ablaze

On April 18, 1906, the cobblestone streets of San Francisco began to roll like turbulent waves on a stormy sea. The 8.3-magnitude earthquake fractured 300 miles (480 km) of the San Andreas Fault, splitting city streets, crumpling trolley tracks, and collapsing buildings block by block. The shaking lasted for almost a full, terrifying minute.

When it was over, nearly all of San Francisco's main water pipelines had broken, leaving the city without a water supply. This would soon prove to be just as disastrous as the shock itself. At the time, most buildings were heated by wood or coal stoves. When the quake struck, it toppled chimneys and stoves throughout the city, sparking dozens of fires. Without water, firefighters and residents could only watch in horror as the downtown area burned. As temperatures climbed to 2,200° F (1,200° C), buildings caught fire just from the heat of flames more than 100 feet (30 m) away.

With its concrete pillars set 12 feet into the ground, the Palace Hotel was supposed to be both earthquake-proof and fireproof. The hotel even had its own water storage tanks, along with 20,000 feet of fire hose and twelve hydrants. But firefighters had to use the water in the tanks to battle blazes on nearby Market Street, so San Francisco's most luxurious building was left to go up in flames.

For three days, the inferno enveloped the city, scorching more than 28,000 buildings over 4 square miles (6 sq. km). In a city of 450,000 people, more than half lost their homes and as many as three thousand lost their lives. After the 1906 quake, the city built new fire stations and a high-pressure back-up water supply with two reservoirs and new pumping stations. But it may not be enough. Today, San Francisco remains at risk for another quake-triggered firestorm because of some of the same factors that contributed to the 1906 disaster. The lack of adequate space between old buildings, and a shortage of fire equipment and personal means the city by the bay is still in danger. One study claims that if another great quake were to hit San Francisco today, the resulting fires could cause up to $5 billion in damages.

Near the corner of 18th Street and Lexington in San Francisco, the earthquake of April 18, 1906, left a long chasm down the middle of the road.

Great Tokyo Fire

When an 8.3-magnitude earthquake struck near Tokyo, Japan, on September 1, 1923, the resulting inferno was even worse than the one caused by the 1906 San Francisco quake. Overturned stoves were mainly to blame for starting more than one hundred fires that soon burned out of control. More than 140,000 people died, many caught in the fire that engulfed the city.

Walls of Water

The most powerful punch in recorded history was packed into the 9.5-magnitude earthquake that pounded southern Chile on May 21, 1960. The pressure had been slowly building along the boundary zone between the South American and Nazca Plates. On that Saturday morning, the surface of the plates began to break free, creating a main shock so large that

scientists believe the shaking traveled more than 3,200 miles (5,100 km) to the core of the Earth. The massive undersea shock triggered tsunamis along the Chilean and Peruvian coasts. Eighty-foot (25-m) waves pounded the coastline, washing away villages and killing hundreds.

Tsunami is a Japanese word meaning "harbor wave." Tsunamis are a series of giant waves triggered by earthquakes, landslides, meteorite crashes, or volcanic activity along the seafloor. In an earthquake, movement along a fault causes the seafloor to buckle. As the stress is released, some of the rock snaps upward, causing huge ripples to flow outward. A tsunami can barrel across the ocean at speeds of up to 600 miles (965 km) per hour, crossing the Pacific Ocean in less than a day.

The tsunamis created by the 1960 quake near Chile were felt across the Pacific Ocean. Fourteen hours after the main

Tuna littered the streets of an Indonesian village after a giant tsunami swept through in 1992.

quake near South America, the tsunami smashed into Hilo, Hawaii, 6,000 miles (9,600 km) away. One of the largest waves, a 20-foot (6-m) wall of water broke through the seawall at Hilo at speeds of more than 400 miles (640 km) per hour and blasted through the downtown area. The Hilo power plant was wiped out, along with numerous cars, buildings, and homes. Sixty-one people died and damages reached more than $20 million. The tsunami continued cutting a path of destruction through the Pacific. Eight hours later, it hit the Japanese islands, flooding coastal villages and killing 185 people. The coasts of California, New Zealand, Australia, and Russia also suffered damage.

Tsunamis can happen in any ocean in the world, but about 80 percent are centered in the Pacific Ocean. This is because of the active plate boundaries, underwater volcanoes, and deep ocean trenches located there. Each year, the Pacific Ocean sees about two tsunamis, with one major tsunami occurring about every decade or so.

In the United States, the National Oceanic and Atmospheric Administration (NOAA) operates the Alaska Tsunami Warning Center and the Pacific Tsunami Warning Center in Hawaii. The center in Hawaii also serves as an international warning center for tsunamis that threaten the entire Pacific Rim. Sensors on the seafloor detect earthquakes and relay the information to ocean buoys, which transmit the data to shore via space satellite communications. Scientists predict the magnitude of the quake, along with where and when the tsunami

Which Wave is Which?

Tsunamis are often confused with tidal waves. But they have nothing to do with tides, which are influenced by the gravitational forces of the Moon, Sun, and planets. Tsunamis are also not storm surges, huge ocean waves caused by violent storms such as hurricanes and typhoons.

Tricky Tsunamis

People are often fooled by tsunamis. Sometimes the series of waves hits land in a short period of time, but other times the waves hit land an hour apart. Many victims, believing the worst to be over, do not wait for authorities to give the "all clear." They return to the beach, only to drown when the next massive wave hits. Also, on the horizon, a tsunami resembles normal waves. Only as it approaches land do the waves slow and compress, growing in height. Swells may reach up to 100 feet (30 m), although most are less than 50 feet (15 m). Never hang around to watch a tsunami. If you can spot the waves, then you are too close.

will hit. The Pacific Tsunami Warning System issues watches and warnings to the public via NOAA weather radio, the news media, and other emergency-response teams. A tsunami watch means a tsunami is possible, while a warning means that one is quite likely or has been confirmed.

The earthquake and tsunami that struck the small Japanese island of Okushiri in July 14 was powerful enough to toss boats ashore and deposit the roof of an inland building on the remains of a wharf.

Recovery workers sift through the wreckage of houses in the village of Lijiang, in the Chinese province of Yunnan along the border with Myanmar (Burma), after an earthquake on February 4, 1996.

Chapter Five

Predicting and Preparing

On February 4, 1975, seismologists in China warned that a major quake was about to hit near Haicheng. Their forecast was based on a number of geologic factors, including ground tilt, changes in groundwater, and a series of **foreshocks**, which are tremors that sometimes occur before the main shock as pressure splits rock. Interestingly enough, scientists indicated that the unusual behavior seen among animals was also a clue. People had reported dogs barking restlessly, farm animals refusing to enter their barns, birds circling without landing, and snakes coming out of hibernation, only to freeze on the surface. Five hours after the prediction was issued, a 7.3-magnitude quake rocked Haicheng. Ninety percent of the city was destroyed.

Earthquake forecasting in China hit a snag when, just one year later, an 8.0-magnitude jolt struck the industrial city of Tangshan, China, 220 miles (350 km) southwest of Haicheng. With no foreshocks or other geological warnings to guide them, scientists could not predict this one. The Tangshan quake officially killed 250,000 people, although unofficial counts put the death toll as high as 650,000.

Since there is no magic formula for determining where and when the next earthquake will strike, the United States Geological Survey (USGS) has never forecasted a major quake. But scientists can make estimates about the future based on what they know about previous quakes, current seismic activity, and plate movement. From satellites in Earth's orbit, the global positioning system (GPS) keeps an eye on the crust, measuring

Seismologist Andrea Donnellan, of the University of California's Jet Propulsion Laboratory, examines a newly installed satellite monitoring station next to the Glendale Freeway in Glendale, California. The station is part of a satellite system that allows scientists to measure even the smallest movements of Earth's crust.

plates and faults as they move inch by inch. Seismologists use the data they collect to calculate the probability, or likelihood, of an earthquake occurring in a particular area.

In Parkfield, California, scientists have set up a variety of sensitive equipment to study a section of the San Andreas Fault that used to shake regularly about once every twenty-two years. (It's been thirty-two years since the last big jolt.) The instruments measure ground tilt, water levels and chemistry, and electromagnetic changes. Lasers send light beams across the fault to record even the slightest motion. **Paleoseismologists**,

Purple laser beams light the night sky near Parkfield, California. The lasers are used by seismologists to detect small movements below Earth's surface.

scientists who specialize in prehistoric earthquakes, dig trenches around the fault. They look at the layers of rock that have built up over the centuries to see when major earthquakes happened in the past. By noting how much time has passed between these quakes, they can get a better idea of when the next big shaker is likely to hit.

Scientists at the USGS figure that San Francisco has a 67 percent chance of being rocked by a great quake sometime in the next thirty years. Similarly, there is a 90 percent chance of a 6.0- to 7.0-magnitude earthquake occurring in the seismically active Mississippi Valley in the next fifty years. As computer technology improves and instruments become more sensitive, perhaps someday seismologists will be able to fore-tell the coming of a force of nature so strong that it can shat-ter a city in mere seconds. Until then, it is important to prepare for the worst.

Bracing for the Big One

Surviving an earthquake often depends on knowing where to build and where not to. In the event of a quake, homes built close to coastlines, rivers, or on floodplains risk damage from liquefaction. Those perched on hillsides may be caught in landslides. Of course, erecting structures near or on a known fault is also unwise. Today, many earthquake-prone cities in the United States do not allow building on sandy soil that may be at risk for liquefaction and landslides. Builders are also required to follow strict building codes, such as using steel reinforcements to bolt building frames to their foundations. Structures are built to sway with seismic waves so they won't crumble during a quake. Still, older homes and businesses built before these codes were put in place remain in danger.

In some countries, such building codes may be nonexistent or not enforced. In August of 1999, a massive quake struck Izmit, Turkey, 55 miles (88 km) southeast of Istanbul. Earth-quakes are common in the region, which sits on the North Anatolian Fault. The 7.4-magnitude jolt reduced Izmit to ruins, leveling nearly 21,000 apartment buildings. More than twenty thousand people died, many suffocating after being

Pedestrians stroll among collapsed buildings and rubble in Sakarya, a town in western Turkey, on August 18, 1999, the day after a powerful earthquake demolished most of downtown and killed 2,000 people.

trapped under the collapsed buildings. Although the government had worked with officials in California to design earthquake-proof structures, many contractors had skimped on construction materials. Lack of enforcement of building codes and corrupt building inspectors also contributed to the disaster.

Quake Mistakes

In the 1995 Kobe quake, numerous buildings constructed atop wet, sandy soil collapsed into the harbor when the soil liquefied. The upper floors of many high-rises also toppled to the ground because of poor building codes that allowed for weaker support beams to be used above the fifth floor.

An aerial view reveals the damage to homes and buildings in the Turkish town of Duzce as the result of an earthquake there on November 13, 1999.

An earthquake survival kit contains such essentials as batteries, a small radio, a flashlight, water, a pocket knife, and basic first aid items.

Since most quake-related deaths are caused by falling debris and the collapse of buildings, it is important to know the right and wrong things to do during a tremor. Since there is a two out of three chance that you'll be at home when an earthquake occurs, here are a few safety tips to keep in mind.

- Know how to shut off the water, gas, and electricity in your home.

- Fasten down pictures, shelves, mirrors, and fragile items with Velcro or museum wax.
- Keep a fire extinguisher in a handy location.
- Find safe zones in your home so you'll know where to go when a quake hits, such as under a sturdy table or next to a wall without windows. Cover your face and head to protect yourself from flying debris and hold on to the furniture.
- Make an earthquake kit. Include enough canned food and water to last for a week, a manual can opener, flashlights, a portable radio, a first aid kit, and pet food. Don't forget the batteries. Update your kit every year.
- Never go outside during an earthquake. If you're outside when one hits, move into the open, away from buildings, telephone wires, and streetlights. Keep away from cliffs, hills, and riverbeds. If you are near a large body of water, get to higher ground.

For more earthquake tips, log on to the Federal Emergency Management Agency's Web site at *http://www.fema.gov* or the American Red Cross's Web site at *http://www.redcross.org*.

Glossary

Alpide Belt—the earthquake-prone zone from Java to the Mediterranean where the Eurasian Plate borders other plates

aftershocks—small-magnitude earthquakes that occur near and after the main shock of an earthquake that may continue for weeks, months, or years

body waves—seismic waves that occur throughout the body of Earth, known as P and S waves

Circum-Pacific Belt—the earthquake-prone region in the Pacific Ocean where the Pacific and other plates border one another; also known as the Ring of Fire

continental crust—the rocky portion of Earth's crust that forms the continents; it may reach as deep as 55 miles (90 km) beneath mountain ranges

core—the central region of Earth that lies below the mantle

creep—slow movement along a fault caused by to the gradual release of stress that tends to produce tiny earthquakes

crust—Earth's outermost; rocky layer

earthquake—vibrations that generate energy in the form of seismic waves caused by rock fracturing within Earth's crust

epicenter—the point on Earth's surface that lies directly above the focus of an earthquake

fault—a fracture in Earth's crust along which two pieces of crust meet

focus—the point of origin within Earth of an earthquake

foreshock—smaller earthquake that occurs before the main shock

intensity—the measure of an earthquake's destruction of human-built structures based on the reports of witnesses and surveys of the damage

liquefaction—a process by which ground shaking causes water-saturated sediment to lose strength and act like a fluid, causing it to sink or float

magnitude—a measurement of the size of an earthquake based on the energy released and measured by the size of the seismic waves created

mantle—the largest layer of Earth's interior, which lies between the core and the crust

Modified Mercalli Intensity Scale—a scale developed by Italian scientist Giuseppe Mercalli that measures the intensity of an earthquake by rating how it was felt on the surface and the amount of damage it caused

moment magnitude scale (Mw)—a scale that measures an earthquake's magnitude based on either a mathematical calculation of the fault rupture or the total energy recorded on a seismogram

oceanic crust—the rocky layer of ocean floor that makes up about 60 percent of the planet's crust and is approximately 3 to 6 miles (5 to 10 km) thick

P waves—the primary, or first, seismic waves from an earthquake that compress and stretch rock

paleoseismologist—a scientist who studies prehistoric earthquake activity

Richter scale—a scale created by professor Charles Richter that rates an earthquake's magnitude based on the strength of its seismic waves

S waves—the slower, secondary earthquake waves that follow P waves, and move the ground up and down and back and forth

sand blows—mounds of sediment and water that explode to the surface, pushed upward by severe ground shaking; also called sand or mud volcanoes

seismic wave—an elastic, invisible wave in rock produced by an earthquake or explosion that travels through rock in all directions; also called a shock wave

seismologist—a scientist who studies and measures earthquakes

seismogram—a written record of ground movements produced by a seismograph system

seismograph—an instrument that produces a chronological record of ground movement during an earthquake

seismoscope—a device that detects ground movement but does not produce a permanent record of it

surface waves—waves produced by an earthquake around the outside of Earth that make the ground shift from side to side and up and down

tectonic plates—the rocky, divided segments of Earth's crust that support continents, islands, and oceans

tremor—a small earthquake

tsunami—a sea wave caused by vertical motion of the seafloor that is caused by fault movement

To Find Out More

Books

Christian, Spencer. *Shake, Rattle, and Roll: The World's Most Amazing Earthquakes, Volcanoes, and Other Forces.* New York, NY: John Wiley & Sons, 1997.

Downs, Sandra. *When the Earth Moves.* Brookfield, CT: Twenty-First Century Books, 2000.

Duey, Kathleen and Mary Barnes. *Freaky Facts About Natural Disasters.* New York, NY: Aladdin Paperbacks, 2001.

Lassieur, Allison. *Earthquakes.* Mankato, MN: Capstone Books, 2001.

Steele, Philip. *Rocking and Rolling*. Cambridge, MA: Candlewick Press, 1998.

Thompson, Luke. *Earthquakes*. New York, NY: Grolier Publishing, 2000.

Videos

Great Quakes, The Learning Channel, 2000.

Natural Disasters, Dorling Kindersley Eyewitness Video, 1997.

The Day the Earth Shook, PBS NOVA, WGBH Video, 1996.

Organizations and Online Sites

Federal Emergency Management Agency (FEMA)
500 C Street S.W.
Washington, D.C. 20472
(202) 646-4600
http://www.fema.gov
http://www.fema.gov/kids
FEMA is a government organization that works to help prevent, prepare for, and assist victims of natural disasters. On the kids page you can find out more about how tsunamis and earthquakes are triggered and learn how to put together your own earthquake survival kit.

National Earthquake Information Center (NEIC)
U.S Geological Survey (USGS)
P.O. Box 25046, DFC, MS 967
Denver, Colorado 80225
(303) 273-8500
http://earthquake.usgs.gov
http://earthquake.usgs.gov/4kids
http://neic.usgs.gov
The United States Geological Survey is a government organization that oversees the National Earthquake Information Center in Colorado. At these web sites you can explore photo galleries, find lists of remarkable tremblers, and discover how seismically active your area is. Check out the USGS kids page for cool earthquake facts, glossary terms, and science fair project ideas. Have a question about earthquakes? Ask a geologist online at *http://ask.usgs.gov*.

University of California at Berkeley Seismological Lab
202 McCone Hall
UC Berkeley
Berkeley, CA 94720
(510) 642-3977
http://www.seismo.berkeley.edu/seismo
Explore some of the myths, misconceptions, and facts surrounding earthquakes and tsunamis. This site also offers resources for teachers and links to other universities and government sites specializing in earthquake information.

West Coast and Alaska Tsunami Warning Center
National Oceanic and Atmospheric Administration (NOAA)
910 S. Felton Street
Palmer, AK 99645
(907) 745-4212
http://wcatwc.arh.noaa.gov/main.htm

The U.S. government's National Oceanic and Atmospheric Administration operates this office and web site, on which you'll find tsunami photos and fascinating facts. Discover why tsunamis are deceptively dangerous and learn tips to help keep you safe when you're near the ocean.

A Note on Sources

My journey into the science of seismology took me to the United States Geological Survey's National Earthquake Information Center in Colorado for research into some of the world's most notable earthquakes, fault movements, and quake measurements. For regional data, I sought out seismology labs at a number of universities, including the University of California at Davis, the University of California at Berkeley, the University of Washington, the University of Alaska, and Michigan Technical University. Further, I relied on the National Oceanic and Atmospheric Administration's Pacific Marine Laboratory in Seattle as well as the Tsunami Warning Centers in Alaska and Hawaii for detailed information regarding tsunami detection and warning.

Books such as David Brumbaugh's *Earthquake: Science and Society*, Philip Fradkin's *Magnitude 8: Earthquakes and Life Along the San Andreas Fault*, and *Disaster! The Great San Fran-*

cisco Earthquake and Fire of 1906 by Dan Kurzman provided scientific and historical perspective. I also tried to read as many books for young readers as possible, rounding out my studies with newspaper reports, magazine articles, and video documentaries.

Many thanks to Dr. Elizabeth Nesbitt, Curator, Geology and Paleontology Division, Burke Museum at the University of Washington, for her wisdom and direction throughout this project.

Finally, growing up and living in earthquake country has given me plenty of first-hand experience with riding out a trembler. Usually, the rumblings that shake the Pacific Northwest are minor ones, like the jiggle that happened during my brother's wedding reception in January of 1995. But some, such as the 6.8-magnitude shocker of February 28, 2001, are enough to send a writer ducking for cover under her computer desk. Because I am frequently reminded of our planet's fiery nature, I also have learned how important it is to be prepared for it. I have an earthquake kit and I know what to do when the ground starts rolling. Make sure you do, too. Your chances of being in a quake are rare, but since you never know when or where the next shaker will hit, be smart—be ready.

—*Trudi Strain Trueit*

Index

Numbers in *italics* indicate illustrations.

About the Author

Trudi Strain Trueit is an award-winning television news reporter, weather forecaster, and freelance journalist. She has contributed stories to ABC News, CBS News, and CNN and has written many books on nature and weather for the Franklin Watts Library Series. Her titles include *Clouds*; *Fossils*; *Rain, Hail, and Snow*; *Rocks, Gems, and Minerals*; *Storm Chasers*; *The Water Cycle*; and *Volcanoes*. Ms. Trueit earned a B.A. in broadcast journalism from Pacific Lutheran University in Tacoma, Washington. She makes her home in Everett, Washington, with her husband, Bill.